MW00910319

FIRST AID
FOR
FIRST YEAR TEACHERS

A Practical Guide for Urban Educators

FATIMA A. MCCARTER

Bloomington, IN Milton Keynes, UK

authorHOUSE

AuthorHouse™
1663 Liberty Drive, Suite 200
Bloomington, IN 47403
www.authorhouse.com
Phone: 1-800-839-8640

AuthorHouse™ UK Ltd.
500 Avebury Boulevard
Central Milton Keynes, MK9 2BE
www.authorhouse.co.uk
Phone: 08001974150

First published by AuthorHouse 5/18/2006

ISBN: 1-4208-7739-9 (sc)

Printed in the United States of America
Bloomington, Indiana

This book is printed on acid-free paper.

This book is dedicated to all of those who

have the courage and passion to teach

In loving memory of my student

Kenneth Dominguez

1988-2005

Dear Reader,

Our youth need teachers like you: A teacher who is passionate, dedicated and motivated to make a difference in the lives of students. Choosing this book shows you possess one or more of these qualities. By opening this book you have demonstrated your readiness to be an empowered and successful teacher.

As a new teacher in an urban school you will face the challenges of working under great bureaucratic constraints and addressing the needs of students who often bring into the classroom the social problems that plaque their inner city community. First Aid for First Year Teachers, (a practical guide for urban educators) was created especially for you. This interactive book is designed to empower and assist you in developing the qualities needed to work with and for young people in your classroom. The focus of this book is to teach you how to manage yourself, develop a better understanding of your students, and build partnerships with colleagues, families and the community.

As you embark on this journey into a field with endless possibilities think about the teachers who have influenced your life, remember your passion and commitment to your students, and remember you are important too!

CONTENTS

BUILD PARTNERSHIPS

AVOID BURN OUT

GOING THE DISTANCE

INTRODUCTION

Teaching sort of fell into my lap. Unlike most of my colleagues, I did not attend college expecting to work in the field of education. Although my mother was a teacher and so was her mother, I had not planned that way. I always had a passion to work with young people, motivating them to do their best. And teaching seemed like the perfect place.

My first year was challenging and full of trial and error. I wanted to be an effective teacher and channeled my energy towards strategies that worked. After my first month, I realized my success as a teacher would require more than theory based education, It meant doing the following:

- Learning about myself and role as an educator.
- Learning about my students and ways to immerse them in learning.
- Building Partnerships with Students, Parents and the Community.
- Learning ways to Avoid Burn-Out.

All of the above are ingredients to empowering you as an educator. It is my hope that you will use this book as a guide and support for you to reference regularly. Congratulations and Continued Success.

KNOW THYSELF

*Knowing others is wisdom, knowing
yourself is Enlightenment*

Lao-tzu

STEP #1
Assess Yourself

Teaching is the most rewarding career that anyone can choose. As a teacher you have the power to shape and mold powerful minds. Watching young people look up to you is inspiring and if you allow it, teaching can give you a sense of belonging and appreciation. It is challenging yet exciting. Teaching is more than a job, it's a passion!

GREAT TEACHERS ARE BORN TO TEACH

Anyone given a curriculum and textbook can teach the content, but it takes someone with a passion for teaching to get students engaged in their learning. Teaching is not only about textbooks. It is bringing the world into the classroom. It is developing lessons to assist young people with the skills they will use – life skills. It's about helping students make connections with the larger community, with their family, most importantly with themselves.

I cannot count for you the number of students who do not believe in their teachers and think teachers come into the school system just to get a paycheck. I find this sad and incomprehensible. Nevertheless, you work in an environment where students often ask why they are in this place called school. You too must examine yourself. Ask the following:

1) Why do I want to teach?
2) How do I feel about young people from diverse backgrounds?
3) What do I expect to get out of this position?
4) How far am I willing to go as an individual/ teacher for my students?

I challenge you to take the time to answer the above questions, sleep on them if you must. Because it would be a grave disservice to you and your students to enter into the teaching profession without the love for it, without the commitment to make a difference, without the passion to create great minds.

EXERCISE #1:
SELF-ASSESSEMENT

Take some time to answer the following questions. Use the space below to jot down your responses.

Why do I want to teach?

How do I feel about young people from diverse backgrounds?

What do I expect to get out of this position?

How far am I willing to go as an individual/ teacher for my students?

What is your mission?

Everyone has some sort of mission in life, whether to rise in the ranks of Corporate America or to own a business. As an educator, you are not exempt from having a mission; in fact you urgently need one. A mission statement represents your values and goals. A mission statement helps you to focus on what you want to do and sets you up to do it. By developing a mission statement, you exhibit your commitment to your career and students. Your mission statement should be in response to the needs of your students and reasonably achievable.

Here's an example:

As an educator, my mission was to teach, empower and assist students in developing the skills needed to achieve academic success.

EXERCISE #2

In the space below, jot down your mission statement

MY MISSION STATEMENT:

Once you have developed your mission statement, you can begin setting goals. Like your mission, goals should be attainable. Do not set goals that are superficial. This could lead to frustration and disappointment. As a first-year teacher, I made the mistake of believing I could make my students read on grade level. My goal was to move my level 1 students to level 4. I soon realized that although I had good intentions, I was unrealistic. I realized that one couldn't go from a level 1 to 4 overnight -it is a process. And with that understanding, I repositioned myself and set goals that were achievable for me and my students.

Tips
- Examine your heart and see where you stand as an educator.
- Develop and convey your mission and goals to your students. Let them know just how interested you are in their education.
- Post your mission and goals.
- Encourage your students to create mission statements of their own. This exercise will help students to look at themselves as individual students.

EXERCISE #3

GOALS FOR STUDENTS

Set at least 3-4 goals each quarter. Remember goals should be realistic and attainable.

FIRST QUARTER
Example: Know the First and Last names of all my students

SECOND QUARTER

THIRD QUARTER

FOURTH QUARTER

PERSONAL GOALS WORK TOO

Setting personal goals are just as important as setting goals for your classroom. I set three-month goals for myself and review them at the end of the third month. You can adopt this habit and encourage your students to do the same.

When I first introduced goal-setting to my students, I had no idea of the impact or excitement it would invoke. My students would set three-month goals such as passing a class they were struggling with, bringing up their grade average or to be a peer mentor. The students worked to reach the goals they set and could hardly wait to review them at the end of the third month. The look on their faces after reviewing accomplished goals is beyond words. They would scream in delight, their faces lighting up with a telling look of satisfaction. If a goal was not met, I encouraged them to ask why and assess how they could achieve it next time. Goal-setting is definitely a lesson you may want to explore.

TIPS
- Begin with the end in mind.
- Become more focused and goal-oriented.
- Set goals that are realistic and attainable.
- Celebrate each time you meet a goal.
- Begin a new goal setting cycle.
- Introduce goal-setting as a lesson.

EXERCISE #4

Set 2-3 personal goals. Remember to review goals at the end of the third month. Celebrate your success.

MY PERSONAL THREE-MONTH GOAL SHEET

September – December
1.
2.
3.

December – March
1.
2.
3.

March – June
1.
2.
3.

June – September
1.
2.
3.

SELF-ASSESSMENT
EMPOWERING STATEMENT

I will be concious of why I am
in this place called school.

I will review my mission statement daily.

I will develop achievable goals and
review them every three months.

STEP #2
Practice Patience

Patience was a virtue I lacked before going into the public school system. I was the person at a red light honking as soon as the light turned and the person in line at the bank huffing and puffing. Once I started teaching, that attitude changed. I came in contact with students who did not read at the same pace as others, students whose challenging behavior would make your jaws clench, and students who were going through that adolescent stage where it was their way or the highway. Boy oh boy, if I did not understand the purpose of patience then, teaching surely put that into perspective. Patience is being calm with your students when things are going haywire. It is taking a step back to realize that some things will happen in due time. Patience is a quality that is learned and if you are anything like me, you will definitely need to practice it.

Tips
- Breathe through a situation.
- Be proactive and not reactive.
- Respond instead of reacting.
- Try to remember things will turn out fine.
- Keep a good attitude.
- Remember patience is a virtue essential for educators.

PATIENCE
EMPOWERING STATEMENT

When things seem to be going
crazy I will breathe.

I will remain calm .

I will take a step back to see
the situation through.

I will respond to the situation
and do what I can.

STEP #3
Humble The Soul

Working in a school system that is struggling to meet the needs of inner city students can be very frustrating. Visitors may come into your classroom and either praise or criticize your teaching tactics. Also, the added pressure of politics in education and meeting standards all could wear and tear on the spirit. Let's face it, the bureaucracy can leave you disillusioned and wondering whether you want to continue teaching. Do not be discouraged. Be humble.

Tips
- Don't allow people to steal your joy.
- Follow wisdom not feelings.
- Do your best.
- Remember your mission.

HUMILITY
EMPOWERING STATEMENT

Words are powerful but I know
how to deal with them.

I will accept praise graciously.

I will accept constructive criticism.

I will not be moved by negativity.

STEP #4
Be Determined

When you decided to teach in an inner city school, some people probably said you were crazy or tried to persuade you to think it would be a waste of time. Those same people may not support your decision but it's not up to them. You matter and what you think is what truly counts. You must be determined to do things that other people say you cannot do. Don't be afraid to step outside of the box. You determine the outcome of your class. If you are determined to succeed, so will your students be.

Tips
- Stay focused.
- Remember you were born to teach.
- Do not let other people's opinions hinder you.
- Remember you can make a difference.
- It takes confidence and determination to fulfill your commitments.

DETERMINATION
EMPOWERING STATEMENT

I will focus on my mission.

I will rememember teaching is my calling.

I will be successful in all that I do.

STEP #5
Be Dependable

Your word means everything and it's all you have. What you say and do will determine how your school year will go with your students. Moreover, it will determine if you are trustworthy. Being dependable shows your students that you care and builds a trusting relationship that fosters education.

Tips
- Don't make promises you can't keep (unrealistic, unethical).
- Be supportive of your students.
- Do the right thing and go the extra mile.

DEPENDABLITY
EMPOWERING STATEMENT

My word is all I have and I will
do my best to keep it.

I will not make promises I cannot keep.

I will be supportive but set clear boundaries.

STEP #6
Be Aware

Teachers are only Human. You have good days and bad days. Pay attention to your feelings. If you are frustrated, know the source of your frustrations. Do not take it out on your students. The classroom should be a safe space for learning.

Tips
- Try to deal with your issues before meeting with students.
- Keep personal and other outside distractions out of the classroom.
- Inform your students if you are not in a good mood, you would be surprised how helpful they can be.

AWARENESS
EMPOWERING STATEMENT

I will pay attention to my life.

I will be aware of how people respond to me.

I will watch how I respond to people.

I will choose to focus on the
positive things in life.

STEP #7
Be Fresh and Enthusiastic

Build up your energy, roll up your sleeves and get ready to work! As an educator, you need to be creative and excited about the lessons you plan to teach. Be involved with the lessons and your students will be sure to follow.

Tips

- Dare to be the one to stand out in the crowd.
- Research and implement exciting and relevant teaching techniques.
- Greet your students with a smile.
- Remember that learning is a life-long process.

ENTHUSIASM
EMPOWERING STATEMENT

I will step out side of the box to teach.

I will put positive energy into
the lessons I teach.

I will use my smile as a motivator.

STEP #8
Be Sensitive

You may work with a population with many barriers against it, such as low-income, undereducated parents, language difficulties or any other hindrances to learning. You must be sensitive to the needs of your students while providing them with a strong education.

Tips
- Educate yourself about the barriers affecting inner-city children.
- Show that you care.
- Be empathetic.

SENSITIVITY
EMPOWERING STATEMENT

I will be conscious of issues affecting
urban students in urban schools.

I will be empathetic.

I will show that I care.

STEP #9
Be A Good Listener

As an educator, active listening is a skill you will have to learn and practice. Active listening shows that you are interested in what your students are saying. This skill will help to build trusting relationships between you and your students.

Tips
- Look at your student while they are speaking.
- Listen not only to the words but the feeling behind the words.
- Be interested in what they have to say.
- Get clarification about what is being said, restate in your own words what your student said.
- Don't interrupt your students when they are trying to tell you something.
- Remember **"God gave you two ears and one mouth." Marva Collins, Educator.**

LISTENING
EMPOWERING STATEMENT

I will be an active listener.

I will listen carefully to what
is said and not said.

I will not listen with defensive ears.

STEP #10
Be Attentive

Working in a classroom with 30 students with different needs can be challenging. Many of your students will be begging for your attention. You may want to pull your hair or   scream. Try not to be overwhelmed.

Tips
- Take long deep breaths and count to three, repeat as many times as needed.
- Set appointments with your students.
- Create a buddy system among your students so learning can be a group effort.

ATTENTIVENESS
EMPOWERING STATEMENT

I will be observant.

I will be courteous and thoughtful
about the needs of my students.

I will manage my classroom time wisely.

STEP #11
Organization is the Key

It is 7:30 in the morning, approximately forty-five minutes before my students arrive. I already have my agenda for the day on the board, the lesson plan on my desk, and the materials I need. As my students stroll in, smiles of good morning light up the classroom and words like" Good Morning Ms" fill the air. I step back to wait for the bell to ring indicating the start of first period and watch my students start their work.

Establishing routines and planning the flow of your day is highly important. When you are organized, your students are better off. Being organized helps to keep you focused and alleviates most classroom management problems. When students walk into your class, they should know what to do, when to do it and how. The classroom environment should be not only inviting but arranged to give your students a sense of belonging.

Tips
- Manage your time wisely.
- Plan ahead.
- Put routines and systems in place that will provide structure.
- Make a daily to-do list.
- Keep a daily log of positive and negative interactions with students.
- File everything.

ORGANIZATION
EMPOWERING STATEMENT

I will create a system that works in my class.

I will plan my activities ahead of time.

I will manage my time wisely.

I will document everything.

STEP #12
Be a Good Student

Learning is a life-long process. It does not matter how many degrees or advanced certificates you have, you do not know everything. Teachers not only teach, they learn. Learn the material you intend to teach inside out. Preparing yourself in advance will help prepare your students for life.

Tips
- Prepare in advance.
- Know your strengths and weaknesses.
- Keep up with educational trends.
- Keep polishing your skills.
- If something is not working, change your approach.
- Remember *"A finished person is a boring person"* - **Anna Quindlen, writer.**

GOOD STUDENT
EMPOWERING STATEMENT

I will build on my strengths.

I will improve my weak areas.

I will keep up with educational trends.

I will learn from my students.

STEP #13
Have a Sense of Humor

My most memorable moments as a teacher are the times I spent laughing. If something funny happened to me, I would tell my students and vice-versa. Having a sense of humor is an absolute must. Try to see the brighter side of a situation and smile.

Tips
- Loosen up.
- Locate your funny bone.
- If you make a mistake laugh and move on.

HUMOR
EMPOWERING STATEMENT

I will have a sense of humor.

I will have a sense of humor.

I will have a sense of humor.

I will have a sense of humor.

NOW SMILE!

STEP #14
Be a Role Model

Believe it or not, your position as an educator is an umbrella that covers more than academics. Your demeanor, attitude and behavior can have a positive or negative impact on your students. You are the adult model your students see everyday. From the way you communicate – words and body language-to the clothing you wear, you are being watched. Remember, you are preparing students for the world.

Tips
- Remember the way you present yourself is a direct reflection of how you feel about yourself.
- Speak articulately to and around your students.
- Maintain a positive attitude.
- Dress professionally.

ROLE MODEL
EMPOWERING STATEMENT

I will present myself in a respectable
and respectful manner.

I will speak positively.

I will model appropriate behavior.

I will be a teacher with great qualities.

KNOW THY STUDENTS

*The greatest good you can
do for another is not just to share
your riches, but to reveal to him his own.*

Benjamin Disraeli, British Prime Minister.

Have you ever seen the movie "Dangerous Minds" starring Michelle Phifer? Just to refresh your memory, Ms. Phifer was a woman eager to teach and was quite excited when she was hired to work as an English teacher. However, when she went to her assigned classroom, she was surprised at what she saw – students throwing paper, talking loudly and playing music. She immediately jumped to the conclusion that she could not teach them. Have you ever jumped to conclusions? We are all guilty of prejudging someone or a situation at one point or another. The question is will you let your fears keep you from doing your life's work? Eventually, Ms. Phifer was able to overcome her fear and, proceeding on faith decided she could make a difference. You can do the same!

CAMERON

Hyperactive, loud and out of control are just a few words to describe Cameron. His loud mouth and disruptive behavior kept him in trouble with most teachers. His mother received frequent phone calls and found herself visiting the school more often than she liked. His report card, colored with red ink from his unsatisfactory behavior, clouded the fact that he was a smart kid who was unsure of himself, unsure of his future.

I was one of the very few teachers able to connect with Cameron. When I looked in his eyes, I saw despair at the same time hope. I made it my business to know his likes and dislikes. I focused more on his likes and interests. I showed him respect and in turn I gained his trust.

Other teachers were not so lucky, I can only guess because they did not take the time to understand him. Very few took the time to have a decent conversation with Cameron to learn more about him. Had they done so, they would have learned that Cameron was smart, funny and charismatic. They would have learned that he loved to write and had the most beautiful handwriting. They would have learned that he moved around a lot with both parents and an older brother until his life was turned upside down when his father was jailed and then his brother. The absence of both male figures and being reared by his working mother left Cameron struggling to fit in.

The circumstances surrounding Cameron's life do not in anyway justify rude or disrespectful behavior but they make you look at the social problems that many inner city kids are faced with.

Cameron is just one of many students who walk into classrooms carrying more baggage than their book bags. An inner-city teacher needs to know the internal and external factors that influence students. Also, it is imperative to know the resources in the community to help with the needs of students. Teaching cannot go on in isolation, nor can understanding students.

STEP #15
Know the Baggage

I am sure you've heard on the news about the many atrocities affecting inner-city youth. From gang violence to illiteracy, inner-city students face many obstacles that can hinder them from succeeding in school.

Tips
- Discuss with students factors that may impact their education.
- Be empathetic.
- Let that baggage be a motivation to succeed.
- Believe that students can always push themselves to be and do more.

STEP #16
Make First Impressions Count

Young people are very impressionable and as the saying goes "the first impression is lasting." It does not matter the grade-elementary, middle and high school students are the same when it comes to the initial meeting. You are the focal point and everything you do and say will hook them or lose them.

Tips
- Greet students with a smile.
- Create pre package folders titled "Welcome to Success," including a letter welcoming them to your class, a letter to parents, emergency forms, etc.
- Give your students some background about yourself.
- Discuss your mission and goals for the class.

STEP #17
Know Each Child

No two people are the same. Every person is unique. Each child is important and comes to you with different needs. You will have students whose reading levels vary or a student who cannot read because of language or other barrier. You will encounter students who need your attention and choose to "act out" to get it or a student who may not say a word. It is your job to know the looks, gestures or remarks students make to tell you what they need.

Tips
- Train yourself to know your students.
- Try to read over students' academic files to get an idea of their strengths and weaknesses.
- Meet with students to discuss strengths and weaknesses.
- Prepare an action plan for each student.
- Everyday is a new day to begin with a clean slate (do not hold grudges).
- Remember **"Every person is equal but not the same."** **Phil Jackson, Basketball Coach.**

STEP #18
Embrace Diversity

We live in a culturally diverse nation, which is the essence of what makes our society so beautiful. Your classroom is only a smaller community. Embrace diversity and you prepare your students with the skills needed to succeed in a diverse nation.

Tips
- Design your classroom with pictures that represent a multicultural environment.
- Discuss diversity.
- If possible, expose students to foods, stories and dances from other cultures.
- Ask students about their culture.
- Celebrate differences.
- Purchase multicultural books and materials.

STEP #19
Preparation is Everything

Students spend just as much time in school as they do at home. School is a home too, and in some instances, the only environment that is consistent with established routines. Preparing your classroom environment for lesson planning should be thought through. Create lessons that are relevant and interactive as well as a classroom environment that give students a sense of belonging.

Tips
- Plan ahead but be flexible.
- Decide on the learning centers you want in your classroom (audio, reading, art).
- Create an environment that is intellectually stimulating, interesting and fun.

STEP #20
Understand the Different Learning Styles

Your students have different learning styles. As an educator, adapting your teaching to different learning styles will help your students learn more effectively. Encourage your students to build on their strengths and improve their weaknesses.

Tips
- Research different learning styles (auditory, visual, kinesthetic).
- Give students self-assessment tests at the beginning of the school year.
- Discuss the different learning styles with students.
- Create lessons that incorporate elements of all learning styles.

STEP #21
Know the Barriers to Learning

Learning disabilities can affect a student's ability to read, write, speak or compute math.

By observing student's academic performance and learning needs, you play an integral role in early identification of learning disabilities.

Tips
- Know what learning-disabled is and is not.
- Pay attention to the red flags(i.e. hyperactive, easily frustrated).
- Keep daily log of students' academic performance.
- Seek training to better assist your students who learn differently.

STEP #22
Awaken Your Students' Enthusiasim

Some of your students are turned off from learning. They have lost hope in our education system and do not see the relevance of school. Those powerful minds have been asleep far too long and it is up to you to wake them up.

Tips
- Turn your students on to learning (knowledge is power).
- Relate school to work.
- Make connections to their lives and the world.
- Help your students to become citizens of the world.
- Challenge students with materials that improve their skills.

STEP #23
Respect Your Students

Your students are human beings who like you deserve respect. And as the saying goes, "You have to give respect in order to get respect."

Tips
- When speaking with your students, maintain eye contact.
- Address students by their first or last name.
- Be careful what you say in words and actions.

STEP #24
Expect Nothing but the Best

Think of yourself as a planter and your students are the seeds. Plant the seeds, cultivate them and watch them grow. Encourage your students to do and produce their best. If they believe a particular assignment does not meet the standards you set in class, give them extra time to create their best work.

Tips
- Condition your students to think positively by planting powerful expectations in those powerful minds.
- Encourage your students to live and learn with expectancy.
- Encourage your students to start acting accomplished.

STEP #25
Promote Self Confidence

I know I can, be what I want to be, If I work hard at it, I'll be where I want to be...

These are the words to a song called "I Can" by Nasir Jones. I remember hearing these words and feeling excited. The song ignites hope in young people and promotes the belief that anything is possible.

Some students may come to you with feelings of worthlessness and insecurity. A good teacher promotes self -confidence, self-reliance and self-respect.

Tips
- Make students feel worthwhile and confident.
- Give students a philosophy for living.
- Speak positive.
- Arm yourself with a book of positive quotations and teach one to your students each day.
- Give them praise (you can do anything you set your mind to do).

BUILD PARTNERSHIPS

"Everyone needs help from everyone"

-Bertolt Brecht

STEP #26
Get a Mentor

I was hired to teach literacy at a middle school in the Bronx, New York. As a part of the district's new teacher initiative, I received training and a wealth of information that would assist me as a first-year teacher. Although I attended orientation during the summer, I was still nervous about teaching a class by myself. The greatest part about it was knowing I was not alone. I was met with open arms of veteran teachers in all subjects. As a new teacher, I was assigned a mentor but took on many mentors who offered their time and assistance whenever I needed it.

Your first year teaching can be scary and difficult. It would be foolish to think that you can wing it alone. Learning about the experiences of veteran teachers who have undertaken this journey can prove invaluable in supporting your first step and later your journey.

Tips
- Observe the veteran teachers in your school.
- Look for someone who enjoys teaching and ask if they would be your mentor.
- Try to gain new insights and ideas.
- Learn first hand what it takes to be a good teacher.
- Discuss the barriers you may encounter.
- Discuss the challenges of being a new teacher.

STEP #27
Get to Know the Teachers in Your School

Getting to know the teachers in your school is very important. This helps to build a sense of community within your school as well as give you an outlet to discuss students you may have in common. As a teacher, knowing your colleagues leaves room for collaborations to be formed and ideas shared.

Tips
- Introduce yourself any chance you get.
- Get involved in positive talk.
- Ask for support when you need it.
- Stay clear of negative talk.

STEP #28
Know the Rest of the Staff

Secretaries, custodians, aides and cooks are all a part of your lifeline within your school. You will definitely need them one way or another.

Tips
- Respect them and their work.
- Know their names-first and last.
- Show them appreciation.

STEP #29
Get Parents Involved

This is probably one of the most important and challenging part of your position. Getting parents involved in their child's education can lead to students' achieving higher grades, completing homework assignments and to positive behavior. By getting parents involved, you show them that you care and want a partnership based on trust and respect. Parents want to feel comfortable knowing that their child is in good hands. They want to feel connected to what is going on in their child's school. Communication is the key in any relationship and ongoing communication with parents will help children learn in and out of school.

Tips
- Make parents feel welcome.
- Learn effective communication strategies.
- Help parents to feel like partners.
- Involve parents with creating an action plan for their child.
- Encourage parents to participate in school activities.
- Use parent conferences as a time to build relationships.

STEP #30
Connect with the Community

To help teach children, schools need support from local communities beyond families. Community leaders and programs can assist with combating the social issues affecting students-alcohol, drugs and violence. When schools, families and communities unite, real progress can be made to educate youth.

Tips
- Identify the community leaders, business owners, and social service agencies in your school district.
- Invite them into your classroom to educate students about what's going on in the community and how they can get involved.
- Learn about youth development organizations that may offer academic and recreational support to your students after school hours.

STEP #31
Become a Member

Do you want to keep abreast of the current trends in education? Well, join an education association. Education associations provide a support system to educators through conferences, online assistance and newsletters.

Tips
- Ask your colleagues about the associations they belong to and how you can get involved.
- Research education associations.
- Attend conferences on education.

AVOID BURN OUT

Life is not complex. We are complex. Life is simple, and the simple thing is the right thing.

- Oscar Wilde

I wanted to do it all. I was going to be the heroine in the story about the teacher who saved all the inner- city children. I was going to be the best teacher no matter what. I would do everything and anything for every last one of my students. I was going to work night and day and stay late at school just so I could feel like I was making a difference. Who cares if I had a thyroid disorder or didn't take care of my health, my job was important and required me to be the best. That was the attitude I had during my first few months on the job. I was neglecting myself and headed towards disaster. It was not until Christmas vacation that I realized I was tired. I mean really tired. I wasn't enthused about the holiday season, I just wanted to lie in my bed, pull the pillow over my head and stay there.

Classroom management, lesson planning, parent meetings, staff development and all the other tasks of a new teacher can be overwhelming. You want to cry, scream, lash out or down right quit. You may find yourself at a point of no return, a point where you are no good to yourself or the people around you. Don't Give Up! I will teach you how to avoid burning out.

STEP #32
Prayer Changes Things

Praying is the driving force that gets me through the day. It is truly about surrendering everything over to a higher power and believing that all things will work out as they should. Praying will be pivotal in avoiding being burnt out. It does not mean you will not be tired because you will. It does not mean you will not be challenged by you students or administration. However, you will know that you walk with the confidence of the most high and he has made it in his plan for you to teach our youth and you will be successful in doing so.

Tips
- Ask God to give you a clean heart each day before walking into your school.
- Ask him to help you be diligent in teaching your students.
- Ask him to show you how to conduct yourself as a role model.
- Ask him to guide and give you the patience needed to work with your students, their family, and your colleagues.
- Tell him you know that you are weak and need him to strengthen you.
- Sit back and watch God work as he uses you to make a difference in the lives of his children.

STEP #33
Love Yourself

When you decided to teach in inner-city schools, you decided you wanted to be of service and give back to the community. Your spirit urged you to reach out and help young people whom most view as a "lost generation." You decided that you wanted to make a difference and give it your all. Teaching must be done with love. If you don't love yourself it will be almost impossible to love your students. It will be impossible to teach with passion and all the other qualities discussed earlier. When you love yourself and exhibit such love, you will do everything in your power to take care of yourself. You will be determined to make sure your needs are met and your space is respected. When you love yourself, you will feel warm on the inside and glow on the outside. Self love really matters.

Tips
- Get in tuned with your spirit.
- Maintain good health.
- Affirm yourself daily.
- Be peaceful.
- Be positive.
- Remember you cannot do everything but you can do something.

STEP #34
Work Smart, Not Hard

For some apparent reason, we as human beings like to make our own lives difficult. We believe that if things are not hard, they are not worthwhile. We want things to be complex, instead of keeping it simple.

Tips
- Keep it simple.
- Establish a routine to ease the work load.
- Do not procrastinate.

STEP #35
Balance Your Life

As a teacher, you will more than likely end up bringing your workload home. Tests need to be graded, lesson plans must be done, and phone calls must be made to parents. All of which are part of being a teacher; However, you must set and maintain boundaries. For instance, if you take work home, do it every other day. Try if possible to keep your weekends for yourself.

Tips
- Know your priorities.
- Give yourself ample preparation time.
- Do not over commit yourself.

STEP #36
Take Time Out

Today was one of your worst days. You were running late only to get to school and find out the teacher with the most challenging class is absent. Your supervisor sends a little note asking you to cover the class during your prep time; on top of that, you received a ticket for not moving your car in time. What do you do?

Things can get pretty hectic at work. But it is your response to what you are experiencing that will determine the outcome of the rest of your day. Take time out.

Tips
- Practice your breathing techniques.
- Have some quiet time.
- Take a walk.
- Listen to soothing music.

STEP #37
Pamper Yourself

I said it before and I'll say it again: Teachers are people too! Sometimes we get so involved in taking care of other people we forget to take care of ourselves. You are important. You are unique. You are a beautiful person who needs some ME time, so why not take it!

Tips
- Do something that brings you joy.
- Give yourself a hug.
- Visit a day spa.
- Exercise.
- Take a day off.
- Attend a personal growth seminar.

STEP #38
Talk About It

By now you should know that teaching is not done in isolation. Everyone needs a support group, whether it's your mentor, colleagues, friends or family. Do not attempt to do it all on your own, use your support group.

Tips
- Ask for help.
- Take a power lunch or dinner to discuss pressing issues.
- Be open to suggestions.

STEP #39
Write About It

We experience things at work or other times in the day and aren't quite sure how to express ourselves to others. Writing about our experiences can be therapeutic and enlightening. You would be amazed at how much you learn about yourself through journaling.

Tips
- Purchase a journal and a special pen.
- Jot down your ideas, thoughts and dreams.
- Try to write in your journal everyday.

STEP #40
Have Fun

Traveling, dancing, roller-skating and reading are all of the things that bring me joy. I make it my business to incorporate these activities into my daily routine in some form or fashion.

Life is beautiful and doing your life's work makes it easy to live. Have fun living. Have fun teaching. Do what ever it is that brings you joy.

Tips
- Get in touch with your inner child.
- Make a list of things you like to do and do it.

STEP #41
Celebrate Success

Celebrate everything -birthdays, completing class projects, even 100% class attendance. It is important to recognize and celebrate the small success stories that add to the bigger picture, your mission statement.

You will succeed at whatever you set your mind to do. If you plan on being a great teacher, you will! If you plan on making a difference in the lives of your students, you will! Remember everything you think about yourself on the inside will manifest on the outside.

Tips
- Celebrate yourself.
- Celebrate your students.
- Invite parents to celebrate with you.
- Teach your students to share each others success.
- Measure your students' success by the small daily victories.
- Take pictures (you always want to capture those great teaching moments).

GOING THE DISTANCE

Great things are not done by impulse, but by
a series of small things brought together.

-Vincent van Gogh

GOING THE DISTANCE

Our youth today are not the same as the youth of yesterday. Times have changed and as an educator keeping abreast to these times are essential. Understanding what you need to succeed is too important to ignore and understanding what your students need to succeed is, well, too important to ignore. The steps I have outlined will set you on a demanding path, however by implementing these steps, you will be able to make a big difference.

Tips
- Don't be afraid to go the extra mile.
- After your first year, become a mentor to a new teacher.
- Continue to further your education (i.e. learn to develop curriculum, get into administration etc...)
- Always be on the look out for new ways of empowering young minds.

THE TEACHERS CREED

I am a passionate teacher
with many fine qualities
I teach outside the box to
immerse my students in
learning

I am dedicated and patient
I am flexible and humble
I have a sense of humor
I am creative
I am dependable

I am a very good student
because learning is a life-
long process
I am supportive and attentive
I am determined and enthusiastic

I am a role model to my students
I embrace diversity
I build partnerships with parents
and other people in the community

I love myself
I love my students
I give respect
I give praise
I AM A PASSIONATE TEACHER!

SUGGESTED READING

Savage Inequalities by Johnthan Kozol

The Essential 55 by Ron Clark

Stories of The Courage to Teach, Honoring the Teachers Heart by Sam M. Intrator

The First Days of School by Wong and Wong

The Gift of Teaching (A book of favorite quotations) Kelly-Gangie & Patterson

Sacred Pampering Principles by Debrena Jackson Gandy

Who Moved My Cheese by Spencer Johnson, MD

Acts of Faith by Iyanla Vanzant

The Prayer of Jabez by Bruce Wilkinson

The Purpose Driven Life by Rick Warren

ABOUT THE AUTHOR

Fatima A. McCarter is the CEO of Youth Transformation Group, an organization committed to empowering and training educators and youth serving organizations, to transform young people to use their talents to maximize the most out of their lives.

She earned her B.A. degree in Sociology from Virginia State University and M.S. in Urban Affairs from Hunter College in New York City. With over a decade of experience in education and human service organizations, Ms. McCarter has remained active in her career, through trainings, management, youth and organizational development.

For First Aid for First Year Teachers (A Practical Guide for Urban Educators) or Youth Transformation Group Services and Product information:
Telephone: 1-862-220-1076

Printed in the United States
202047BV00005B/7-9/A

9 781420 877397